GERVASE PHINN

Happy Days

First published in 2017 by Country Publications Ltd
The Water Mill, Broughton Hall
Skipton, North Yorkshire BD23 3AG
www.dalesman.co.uk

ISBN 978-1-85568-362-4

Printed in Europe for Latitude Press Ltd.

Introduction

Happy Days is a personal collection of anecdotes, reminiscences, observations and opinions on the theme of happiness. At a time when the newspapers and the television focus relentlessly on tragedies, disasters, terrorist atrocities and distressing events, perhaps this book is timely. We need to be reminded that there is still a great deal of happiness in the world; there are still amusing, good-hearted and compassionate people who brighten our lives; there are still times when we delight in the things around us.

In compiling this anthology I have described some of the occasions that make or have made me happy, and also

included the thoughts and feelings of others. Many of the contributions from family friends and readers of my books had me smiling and not a few had me laughing out loud.

There are so many occasions when one is filled with a feeling of great elation: the birth of a child, a christening or wedding, a childhood holiday, a celebratory birthday or a cosy family Christmas... these are the magical memories that stay with us all our lives.

Sometimes it is the small things in life that make us happy: seeing a rainbow, sitting with family members and going through old photographs, meeting a friend you haven't seen for years, receiving a compliment or a word of thanks, seeing a wood full of snowdrops, listening to a piece of music, watching a play, a tender kiss.

One very happy memory of mine was visiting my Grandma Mullarkey. I looked forward to those visits because she took a particular interest in my reading and writing. I cannot pinpoint the precise moment when I came to the decision that I wanted to be a writer, but certainly on those occasions when I sat with my grandmother listening to her stories and anecdotes, her reminiscences and commentaries, the seed was sown. I will leave you with her favourite Irish blessing:

May flowers always line your path, and sunshine light your day.
May songbirds serenade you, every step along the way.
May a rainbow run beside you in a sky that's always blue,
And happiness fill your heart each day your whole life through.

GERVASE PHINN

Contents

Special delivery

The new baby

Surely the happiest time for parents is the arrival of their new baby. After months of waiting — swollen ankles, morning sickness, fatigue, cravings, sleepless nights, cramps, food aversions, headaches, constipation and mood swings (and that's only the father) — the great day thankfully arrives. All the trauma seems to have been forgotten by the mother as she nurses her baby at her breast. Nothing in the world compares to the sight of the newborn baby taking his or her first breath.

As I awaited the arrival of Richard, our firstborn, the Scottish sister in charge of the maternity ward told me in no uncertain terms that if I wished to attend the birth,

---

Out of the mouths of babes and sucklings. — Old Testament

I was not to get in her way; and should I faint, I would not be attended to: I would be left on the floor. The mother was more important and Sister McLaren couldn't be bothered with me.

When I assured her that I would not faint she gave a wry smile. "Bigger men than you have keeled over," she told me. This was followed by a shake of the head and the usual time-worn comment that if men had to have babies there'd be no children in the world.

When Christine's time came for the birth I stood at the head of the bed, shouting in her ear at intervals: "Breathe, breathe! Push! Push!"

Sister McLaren took my arm. "If you don't stop that dreadful noise immediately, you can push off. Stand over there and be quiet."

I felt like a naughty schoolboy.

Before you were conceived I wanted you.
Before you were born I loved you.
Before you were here an hour I would die for you.
This is the miracle of life.

Maureen Hawkins

"And what have you been learning at school then?" the school inspector asked the small boy.

"Not much," the child answered. Then after a thoughtful pause, he announced, "I do know how to mek babies, though."

The visitor tried not to look in the least shocked and replied in a very casual voice, "Really?"

"Aye I do. I've just learnt how to mek babies." He gave the inspector an old-fashioned look. "Do you know how to mek babies, then?" he asked.

"I do, yes," the important visitor replied.

There was another long pause. "How do you mek babies, then?" the boy asked, looking the inspector straight in the eye.

"You go first," he was told.

"Well," he said, looking up at the cloudless blue sky. "I knock the 'y' off and add 'i-e-s'. Is that how you mek babies, then?"

God mark thee to His grace! Thou was the prettiest babe that e'er I nursed. And might I live to see thee married once, I have my wish.
William Shakespeare, from *Romeo and Juliet*

The Day Mum Brought the Baby Home

When Mum brought the baby home,
Everyone forgot about me.
Grannie cooed, "Ooooo, isn't she bootiful?"
Grandpa cried, "Ehhhhh, isn't she luvverly?"
Auntie Christine sighed, "Ohhhhh, isn't she
gorrgeous?"
Uncle Michael chortled, "Ahhhhh, isn't she
amaazing?"
Even the brothers said, "Wow, isn't she cool?"
Then they looked in my direction.
I said to them all, "Are you asking me?
Because if you are, I don't agree.

She has no teeth, is bald and fat.
I'd sooner have a dog or cat.

---

that you never knew was empty.

Well, they don't dribble down your clothes,
Poke your eyes and squeeze your nose,
Slather, gurgle, drool and slurp,
Slobber, bubble, spit and burp,
Wet tons of nappies all the time,
And scream and mewl and moan and whine."

Everyone looked shocked.
"I thought you'd love your little baby sister,"
said Dad sadly.
"I do love her," I replied, smiling,
"I'm just trying to get a bit of attention around
here, that's all!"

I love children. Especially when they cry
— for then someone takes them away.
Nancy Mitford

I received a letter recently from a proud new father saying how indebted he was to me. He explained:

"My wife was in the maternity ward at the hospital awaiting the arrival of our first child. The baby was overdue and the doctor informed her that the following morning the baby would have to be induced. She was not keen on having any drugs and did not want the baby to be induced, but the doctor informed us that it would be dangerous if the child was left in the womb any longer. We reluctantly agreed, but my wife was distressed and that evening she shed a few tears. The nurse gave her a book by Gervase Phinn to take her mind off things and hopefully cheer her up. My wife laughed so much at one of the anecdotes that it brought the baby on and she was delivered of a healthy boy without the help of any drugs. We are so very grateful."

I wrote back and asked if he had called the baby after me.

He replied, "We're not that grateful!"

Honey is sweet. A little baby is even sweeter. — Asian saying

Here is the anecdote that caused so much amusement:

At morning break, Mrs Brown told me that John, one of her pupils, lived on a farm way out across the moors. It was a hard but happy life he led. He was expected, like most children from farming families, to help around the farm — feed the chickens, stack wood, muck out and undertake a host of other necessary jobs, and all that before he started his homework. He was a shrewd, good-natured, blunt-speaking little boy with a host of stories to tell about farm life.

When he was little, Mrs Brown told me, he had been awakened by his father one night and taken into the byre to see the birth of a black Angus calf. The vet had suggested

The quickest way for a parent to get a child's attention is to sit down and look comfortable.
Lane Olinghouse

---

that it was about time the boy saw this miracle of nature. John had stood on a bale of hay in the cattle shed, staring in the half-light as the great cow strained to deliver her calf. The small, wet, furry bundle soon arrived, and the vet, wet with perspiration and with a triumphant look on his face, had gently wiped the calf's mouth and then held up the newborn creature for the little boy to see. John had stared wide-eyed.

"What do you think of that?" the vet had asked him. "Isn't that a wonderful sight?"

John had thought for a moment before replying. "How did it swallow the dog in the first place?" he had asked.

Sign outside the Royal Infirmary Maternity Unit:
"For deliveries, please use the back entrance."

"The doctor's been and everything is fine," said the nurse to the new father. "Mother and baby are doing very well, so you can take them home when you're ready. Now, do try to encourage your wife to persevere with the breast-feeding. The baby hasn't made a good start but will soon get a taste for mother's milk and then there'll be no stopping him."

As the new mother was packing the few things she had in her bedside cabinet, her husband picked the clipboard off the bottom of the bed. The sheet of paper attached to it had the mother's name and the baby's and other details. Below was the section headed Doctor's Comment.

"May I have this, please?" asked the father.

"Why do you want it?" asked the nurse.

"I want to keep it until my son is twenty-one," she was told, "and on that birthday I want to present it to him in a gilt frame, saying: 'When I am dead and gone, perhaps you

---

Parenthood is a unique journey that not

might sometimes look upon that scrap of paper in the golden frame and remember this very special day, your coming of age, and I hope you might remember a father and a mother who were so very proud of you and loved you more than any other parents loved a son. You see, it's the first thing anybody wrote about you.' I shall tell him, 'It is the doctor's comment written during your first week of life.' You see, nurse, that is why I want to keep this sheet of paper."

"Oh," she said. "How lovely. You're making me cry. And what does the doctor say?"

Smiling, he passed over the piece of paper so she could read what the doctor had written: "Poor sucker".

A new baby is like the beginning of all things — wonder, hope, a dream of possibilities.
Edna J Le Shan

---

everyone has the good fortune of experiencing.

"Ooo, who's a pwetty baby?
Oh, who's an ickle lamb?
A pint-sized bobby dazzler,
Gurgling in your pram?
With your ickle tiny fingers,
And your ickle tiny toes,
And your bootiful big blue eyes,
And your cutey-tootie nose.
You're Grannie's ickle poppet,
A coochi-coochi coo,
Grannie's ickle pwincess,
A bubbly, wubbly woo."
Then sitting up, the baby,
She spoke unto her gran,
"I think it might be better
If you *got in the pram."*

Babies are like little suns that, in a magical way,

In the delivery room was a giant mirror on wheels so if the mother-to-be wanted to, she could watch the delivery.

One particular mother asked the nurse to wheel it over.

"I guess you wish to watch the delivery," said the nurse.

"Heck, no," replied the woman. "I want to check my hair."

I have to admit that I had a very easy time when my children were babies. I was never called upon to feed them because Christine breast-fed all four. When she got up in the night to see to the crying baby, I slept on soundlessly. I also had the good fortune of having a wonderful mother-in-law who arrived soon after the birth and took charge: cooking, cleaning, washing and looking after my wife.

---

bring warmth, happiness and light into our lives.

But then, when Matthew (Baby Phinn No2) arrived just before Christmas, my in-laws decided to go on a cruise and I was on my own. I had to write the cards, buy the presents, do the cooking and cleaning, water the plants and tackle numerous other chores.

I was halfway through washing the nappies (we had the old-fashioned towelling variety, none of your disposable types used today) when a voice came from upstairs.

"Could you fetch the baby please?" shouted Christine. "He needs feeding."

Just for a bit of a wheeze, I wrapped the turkey in the baby's shawl and took that up instead of the baby. Christine opened the shawl to find this frozen turkey.

"Where's the baby?" she screamed.

"Oh gosh!" I said. "I must have put him in the oven."

The health visitor did not see the funny side. "You silly man!" she cried. "You could have dried your wife's milk up."

Children refresh the life and rejoice the heart.

Sister Mullarkey was in charge of our local maternity ward. In her long career she had supervised many a birth. One mother, a fair-complexioned young woman, gave birth to a healthy boy with a head of black curly hair and very dark skin. Her husband, also a fair-complexioned man with wavy blond hair, paced outside in the corridor awaiting news. The new mother, presented with her baby, stared at the small bundle in her arms, stared at the small face and then burst into tears.

"Perhaps I should look after the baby until you have had a word with your husband," the sister suggested tactfully.

Upset that baby number four was another girl, the father threw his hands up in the air and announced, "As soon as we leave here, we're trying again!"

The mother yelled back, "Oh, yes? You'll be doing it alone then!"

A babe in the house is a well-spring of pleasure,

It was the start of the new term after the Christmas holidays. The children, aged eleven, were keen to tell their teacher about the presents they had received. One girl explained that there was an unexpected present in her home over the festive season.

"Miss, Miss!" the girl shouted out, waving her hand in the air like a daffodil in strong wind. "My sister had a baby on Christmas Day."

"Your sister had a baby?" said the teacher, startled.

"Yes Miss. It were a little boy," the girl told her, jumping to her feet. "She didn't know she was having it and nobody else did either. Mam and Dad had gone to the pub in the afternoon, and I had to stay in with my sister because she wasn't feeling too well. Anyway, when my mam and dad had gone out she felt funny and the next thing what happened was she flopped on the settee and all this water come out over the floor and she started moaning and groaning."

---

a message of peace and love. — Martin Farquhar Tupper

The rest of the class sat in stunned silence during what could only be described as a performance as the girl related the facts in graphic detail and at great speed, illustrating her account with facial expressions and actions. There wasn't a sound. Some children shuffled in embarrassment, others stared at her uncomprehendingly, some pulled faces and others sat open-mouthed. The girl rattled on regardless, with ruthless directness and in a voice strong and determined.

"Anyway, I thought she were really ill," the girl told her audience. "My sister kept holding her stomach like this. 'Oh!' she went, 'I feel awful.' Then she told me to go and fetch Mrs Lloyd who lived next door. She was a middlewife and used to deliver babies. Anyway she weren't happy having to leave her Christmas tea and told me to go for the doctor and I told her I had done but he was out. Then she phoned for an ambulance but they said it would be ages coming because of the snow and the roads being icy and all and it being Christmas Day as well so she said she'd come with me. When we got home my sister was stretched out on the living room floor moaning and groaning and saying she was going to die. Nurse Lloyd looked at her and told me to get some towels and boil some hot water and then she told me to hold my sister's hand to calm her down because she was moaning and groaning something rotten. Then the baby just popped out. There was lots of blood." A ginger-headed boy in front gave an involuntary shudder and there were several sharp intakes of breath. "I think Mrs Lloyd was mad with the baby because she slapped it on its bum and it started roaring its eyes out. Then this play centre come out."

"Play centre?" repeated the teacher.

"It's all this gooey stuff what comes out after the baby."

"Ah, the placenta," mouthed the teacher.

---

usually don't have one. — Leo J Burke

"And it was fastened to a long sort of cord."

"What, the play centre?" asked the ginger-headed boy, saucer-eyed.

"No, it was fastened to the baby. It's called the umbrella cord and Mrs Lloyd had to cut it. She knew what she was doing because she was a middlewife. Mrs Lloyd wrapped the baby in a towel and gave it to my sister. Then the ambulance come and I went to fetch my mam and dad from the pub and we all went in to the hospital to see the baby. It was put in an incinerator." The girl turned to the class. "If anyone has any questions, I'll answer them." There was a bewildered silence in the classroom.

"I don't think we'll have questions, thank you," said the teacher, quite at a loss for what else to say.

"Miss," said the ginger-headed boy, "I got a play centre for Christmas."

Be gentle with the young. — Juvenal

"I baptise this child"

Christenings

A christening or baptism service is a joyous occasion. The child, often a newborn baby, is given to God as a sign of faith by his or her parents, who vow to raise their son or daughter in a Christian home. There are very few life events so important and so heart-warming as a christening, and inevitably careful planning is involved. The principal decision of the baby's parents is to choose the godparents, who will be prepared to encourage their godchild to develop Christian values — being kind and compassionate towards others, and standing against things in the world that cause injustice and suffering. They pray that the child will grow up healthy, happy and loving.

Little children head-ache;

The Irish Blessing for the Christened Child

May the strength of the wind and the light of the sun,
The softness of the rain and the mystery of the moon
Reach you and fill you.
May beauty delight you and happiness uplift you,
May wonder fulfil you and love surround you.
May your step be steady and your arm be strong,
May your heart be peaceful and your word be true.
May you seek to learn, may you learn to live,
May you live to love, and may you love, always.

The church or chapel is booked, the guests invited and the reception organised, the baby is dressed in sparkling white. Well, this is not always the case. In my own family, as in many others, the baptismal gown (now rather yellow and worse for wear) has been passed

---

big children heart-ache. — Italian proverb

down from previous generations and has been worn by myself, my children and my grandchildren. I recall my eldest son Richard, aged eight, asking when his baby sister Elizabeth was baptised, "Why is Lizzie wearing that tatty old dress?"

Another big decision taken by the parents before the special day is to decide on the Christian name for the child. My parents clearly had a sense of humour, calling a boy born in Rotherham Gervase. The name comes from a

Sometimes the smallest things take up the most room in your heart.
Winnie-the-Pooh

The six-year-old girl sat with her grandmother watching the christening of her baby brother. She stared intently as the minister poured water over the baby's head and then asked her grandmother, "Why is that man brainwashing the baby, Grannie?"

Norman French form of the Old Germanic name *Gervas*, said to mean 'spear servant' from *ger* (spear) and *vass* (servant). The name was introduced into England by the Normans and was relatively common for a few centuries. The blacksmith in *The Miller's Tale*, the rudest and funniest story of Chaucer's epic poem *The Canterbury Tales*, is a Gervase. Most people have never heard of the name and over the years I have collected a delightful range of

---

— and never outgrows it. — Frank A. Clark

inventive guesses that have appeared on my letters. They range from 'Grievous Pain' to 'Gracious Dhin'. I have been called 'Germane', 'Germain', 'Germinal', 'Gercase', 'Jarface', 'Gerund', 'Garfase' and even 'Geraffe'.

When asked by the visiting minister, who was taking the school assembly, what a christening was like, one child answered, "It's a bit like dunking a biscuit in a cup of tea".

When visiting schools, I have come across children with more unusual names than mine. Some are named after the children of pop stars, footballers and film and television personalities — names like Apple, Audio, Bronx and Coco.

A vicar told me, "The old biblical names seem to be fast disappearing. Samuel and Simon, Mary and Michael,

Joseph and James are now replaced by Dean and Darren, Carlie and Crystal, Shane and Sharlene. Some parents give precious little thought to the fact that their children, when they arrive at school, have to cope with some quite bizarre names. One parent, evidently somebody who liked cowboy films, was quite intent on calling his twin girls Cheyenne and Sioux. I've been asked to christen Rainbow, Bliss, Marvel and Maximus. I drew the line when asked to christen a child Kipper. I've had requests for Jezebel and Salome and Delilah. It's difficult explaining to the parents who these women were and what their line of work was."

He continued, "One child very nearly went through life with the exotic name of Onacardie. I asked the parents at the christening: 'And what is the name of the child?' The mother replied loudly, 'It's Onacardie.' I had just begun sprinkling the water over the baby's head and intoning, 'Onacardie, I baptise you in the name of the Father and of

---

life should go on. — Carl Sandberg

the Son and of the…' when I was interrupted. 'No, no, vicar!' the mother hissed. 'On 'er cardy. The name's written on her cardigan. She's called Siobhan'."

"A christening," the vicar told the young father, "is a very serious occasion. Are you fully prepared for it?"

"Oh yes," replied the father. "We organised everything. There's a reception back at the house with plenty of food."

"I am not talking about food," said the vicar tersely. "I mean, are you fully prepared spiritually?"

"Oh yes," replied the young father. "We've a good selection – whisky, gin, brandy…"

If men had to have babies, they would only

The vicar was conducting an assembly and was telling the children about Adam and Eve and the concept of Original Sin.

The babe, with a cry brief and
dismal,
Fell into the water baptismal;
Ere they'd gathered its plight,
It had sunk out of sight,
For the depth of the font was
abysmal.

EDWARD GOREY

"Some of you," he said, "when you were little babies, came into St Margaret's Church all dressed in white with your mums and dads and with your god-parents. It was such a very, very special and very happy occasion. I took you in my arms, carried you gently to a large stone bowl called a font and I did something to you." The headteacher raised an eyebrow. "I expect," continued the clergyman, "that you children know to what I am referring. I wonder if anyone can tell me what

---

ever have one each. — Diana, Princess of Wales

I did to you when you were a baby?" His question was met by silence. "Well, let me give you a little clue. The word begins with a curly 'c'. What did I do to you that begins with the letter 'c'?" Again there was silence. He seemed to be getting nowhere; however, he persevered. "The word begins with the sound 'chr—'?"

It was a little boy who raised his hand.

"And what is the word," the clergyman asked the child, "beginning with the sound 'chr—', something that I did to you when you came to my church as a baby?"

The little boy replied, "Crucify."

Children begin by loving their parents; as they grow older they judge them; sometimes they forgive them.
Oscar Wilde

Having a baby is like getting a tattoo on your face. You really need to

However meticulously planned, a christening can sometimes go wrong, as these accounts testify:

Kieran was like a little devil at his christening (perhaps not the best simile given the occasion). He wriggled and cried and screamed and flailed his arms when the priest took him from his mother. There was no way he was going to get dunked in cold water and resisted all attempts. The embarrassed father apologised for his baby son's behaviour.

"Sure, don't go worrying your head about that," the priest replied. "Your son is destined for great things. They say that the wildest colts make the best horses" — at which point the baby gave the priest a hefty kick.

After the baptism, the five-year-old brother of the baby was unusually quiet.

"Is something wrong?" asked his father.

be certain it's what you want before you commit. — Elizabeth Gilbert

The child nodded solemnly.
"Well, what is it?" he was asked.
"The priest said he wanted Joseph to be brought up in a Christian home. I want him to stay with us."

During the christening there was some consternation around the font. The baby girl, about to be baptised, was taken from the priest. There were whispered conversations and embarrassed faces. The mother whisked the baby away and disappeared with her into the

I can't say that I was a wanted child. The vicar poured boiling water over me at my christening.
Les Dawson

presbytery. The baby's brother, a child of eight, who had been standing by the font watching proceedings, announced to the congregation in a loud voice: "She'll be back soon. Mum's gone to change her. She's just done a Number Two."

The seven-year-olds were asked by their teacher to write about what they did at the weekend. One small girl wrote: "We went to church to see my baby brother advertised".

A little boy witnessed for the first time the rite of baptism. He was fascinated and the next morning his parents found him pouring a jugful of water over the head of the cat. He explained to his angry mother that he was baptising it.

---

was glad to get him asleep. — Ralph Waldo Emerson

As soon as the happy gurgling baby was passed by her mother into the priest's arms, the child uttered the most deafening scream and writhed and wriggled and kicked. The baby continued in this manner for the entire service, her voice reaching a crescendo when the cold water was poured on her head. Coming out of the church, the embarrassed father turned to one of the godparents.

"I don't know about a christening," he remarked. "It was more like a bloody exorcism!"

A curious six-year-old who had watched with great interest the baptism of her baby brother by the woman priest was overheard asking her father on leaving the church: "What was all that about then? Was that woman trying to drown the baby?"

Babies are such a nice way to start people. — Don Herold

For better, for worse

Weddings

A wedding should be the most wonderful day in a bride and groom's life. For the happy couple, who commit themselves to spending their lives together, it promises to be the most significant decision they are ever likely to make. When the two people take their vows, they leave behind the past and look forward to a bright new life together.

For many, there are months of meticulous planning involved before the special day. The best man, groomsmen and bridesmaids are chosen, the church or register office booked, the hotel reserved, the menu decided upon, the guest list compiled, the cake ordered, the bride's dress

---

Marry first and love will follow. — proverb

bought, the readings selected, and countless other things, including the bride deciding what to wear to bring her good luck on her special day.

"Something old,
Something new,
Something borrowed,
Something blue
And a silver sixpence in her shoe."

The old item provides protection for the baby to come; the item borrowed from another happy bride means good luck; the colour blue is a sign of fidelity; and the sixpence is a symbol of prosperity and acts as a ward against evil done by any frustrated suitors.

At my daughter's wedding, Elizabeth wore her grandmother's Victorian brooch (something old), diamond studs, a gift from her parents (something new), her mother's emerald ring (something borrowed) and a ribbon

---

Marry in haste and repent at leisure. — proverb

from a close friend (something blue), which she pinned to her underwear.

When discussing her wedding with my eldest son Richard, Nina, his fiancée, asked if I might pen a poem in celebration of the occasion. "Something about love and family, about care and compassion," she said.

At the wedding reception, following the speeches by the best men (Richard's two brothers), the father of the bride and the groom, I was called upon to declaim the verse I had written especially for the happy event. I prefaced the

If you're thinking of getting married, you might as well learn right now that you have to let women be women.
from *Hello Dolly*

The highest happiness on earth is the

recitation by repeating Nina's words and, after a dramatic pause and to a hushed audience, I began...

When I am old!

When I'm old and wrinkly, I shall not live alone
In a pensioner's flat or an old people's home,
Or take an apartment on some distant shore.
I'll move in with my son and my daughter-in-law.

I'll return all the joy that my son gave to me
When he sat as a child on his dear father's knee.
He will welcome me willingly into his home
When I'm old and I'm wrinkly and all on my own.

I'll spill coffee on the carpet, leave marks on the wall,
I'll stagger home drunk and be sick in the hall.
I'll sing really loudly and slam every door,
When I live with my son and my daughter-in-law.

---

happiness of marriage. — William Phelps

I'll rise from my bed in the late afternoon,
Throw the sheets on the floor and mess up my room.
I'll play ear-splitting music well into the night,
Go down for a snack and leave on every light.

I'll rest my old feet on the new leather chairs.
I'll drape dirty underwear all down the stairs.
I'll talk to my friends for hours on the phone
When I live with my son in his lovely new home.

I'll come in from the garden with mud on my shoes,
Flop on the settee for my afternoon snooze,
Expect that my tea will be ready by four
When I live with my son and my daughter-in-law.

I'll leave all the dishes piled up in the sink
And invite all my noisy friends round for a drink,

I'll grumble and mumble, I'll complain and I'll moan
When I'm old and I'm wrinkly and all on my own.

I'll watch television hour after hour,
And I'll not flush the toilet or wash out the shower.
Oh, bliss, what a future for me is in store
When I move in with my son and my daughter-in-law.

The happy couple moved to Bermuda!

The vicar spent rather too long in his marital address to the congregation, which was getting impatient. After a while one of the small bridesmaids sitting on the front pew announced in a loud voice: "Mummy, when will they pay that man to shut up?"

---

which always seems too short. — André Maurois

The priest officiating at the wedding was rather worse for drink and in his homily concerning the Marriage Feast at Canaan in Galilee, he informed the congregation that when Jesus turned the wine into water it was a miracle. Realising his faux pas, he corrected himself. "I mean the water into wine," he said, laughing, and then added, "I don't suppose that turning the wine into water would have gone down all that well."

We're having a little disagreement. What I want is a big church wedding with bridesmaids and flowers and a no-expense-spared reception and what he wants is to break off our engagement.
Sally Poplin

Marry in Lent and live to repent. — proverb

The greatest fear of any bride and groom is that things will go wrong at the wedding: the bride is ill, the reception has been double-booked, the cake doesn't arrive, the photographer forgets, the best man gives a vulgar speech, an uncle settles old scores with a relative. A marriage is what brings family and friends together, and when people are brought together, disasters sometimes occur: people get drunk, have arguments, they cry, throw tantrums, fight, and make what should be a delightful and memorable day into a catastrophe. Despite all the months of detailed planning, things can go wrong, as these stories testify:

The bride and groom arrived at the reception and walked past a row of guests who cheered and showered them with confetti. One elderly relative, a little worse for drink,

---

Marry the daughter on viewing the mother. — proverb

became confused and, instead of throwing confetti, flung her champagne over the happy couple.

"I was invited to the wedding of a work colleague and received the wedding list. It included a flat-screen television, a dishwasher, a dining table, a full set of crystal glasses and a laptop computer. She got a cheeseboard."

A delighted incredulous bride
Remarked to the groom at her side:
"I never could quite
Believe till tonight
Our anatomies would coincide."
anon

Marriage has many pains but

On the morning of the wedding, she was in a complete panic. She said, "Something old, something new — I've got nothing borrowed and blue!" I said, "You've got a mortgage and varicose veins, will that do?"

Victoria Wood

The three-year-old page boy announced loudly as the bride and groom were about to take their vows: "I need a poo!"

The bride's brother fancied himself as something of a singer and thought the wedding would be an ideal opportunity to show off his talents. At the reception he began serenading his sister with a song he had composed

---

celibacy has no pleasures. — Dr Johnson

himself. It was called something along the lines of *Love You Forever*, and was embarrassingly bad with banal lyrics and a monotone of a tune. Worse was that he had a high, nasal voice which was off-key. The song went on for a good few verses before the father of the bride, seeing the expressions on the faces of the guests, plucked the guitar from his son's hand and said loudly, as if talking to a child, "That's quite enough, Gavin. I think we've all heard enough."

It is the custom that a woman's name changes on her marriage. Crystal Morris decided to keep her maiden name when she married Dennis Ball and Holly Mason to keep hers when she married James Berry.

It was a very posh affair held in a stately home. The parents of the bride had spared no expense. The setting

was magnificent, the weather was glorious, the men on the bride's side were dressed in morning suits, the women in beautiful expensive-looking dresses. It was clear the people of the groom's side were of a very different class. Some of the men had had too much to drink. Some of the women were raucous. The guests had gathered in the gardens with their Pimms and canapés when the father of the groom appeared and shouted, "Can you all shift your arses? T' meal's ready."

"In his spare time my husband is a children's entertainer and uses a large puppet called Bobby to amuse the little ones at birthday parties. At our wedding he waited at the altar with Bobby, the puppet, dressed like him in an identical wedding

---

outfit. When the vicar asked my husband-to-be if he would take this woman to be his lawful wedded, he answered 'I do'. Then Bobby said, 'I do as well'."

The wedding reception had ended and the newlyweds had just gone off to the honeymoon suite. After a champagne supper the groom retired to the bedroom, but the bride went out on to the balcony and sat there, gazing at the stars. "Aren't you coming to bed, dear?" asked the impatient husband. "No," she announced. "My mother told me this was going to be the most beautiful night of my life, and I don't want to miss a single minute of it."

"Her two bridesmaids were large ladies and would no doubt have been an asset as prop forwards for Wigan. Both were heavily

---

same things you do. — J D Salinger

muscular. One had a fake moustache and a duelling scar. The room where they held the wedding reception had all the intimacy of Lenin's Tomb on half-day closing. Cheap sherry was served in cracked tumblers. God knows who trod the grapes for the tepid brew, but in my glass I found a Spanish corn plaster."

Les Dawson

Once, when I was on stage at a theatre show at which my wife of forty-four years, sitting on the front row, attended, I asked Christine: "Could you, in your wildest dreams, imagine that when you married me, I would be doing this for a living?"

Her answer was swift: "You are never in my wildest dreams," she replied.

Ah, such is married bliss!

Unequal marriages are seldom happy. — Scottish proverb

Thankyou very much
for the lovely wedding present.

Are we nearly there yet?

Holidays

I guess for most of us the annual holiday must be one of the happiest times in our lives, when we take a break from the tedium of school or the grind of work. How we look forward during the year to one or two weeks' respite, to relax around a swimming pool, bathe in the sea, take a brisk walk along a promenade breathing in the fresh salty air, eat out; or maybe fly to faraway places we have always wanted to visit.

Most summers, when Steel, Peech and Tozer, the foundry where my father worked, had its 'shut-down week' and the furnaces were cleaned, the Phinn family had its fortnight in Blackpool. For my parents it must have been

---

Business is so bad at that hotel, they're

such a treat to break from the routine of work, an opportunity for them to recharge their batteries and enjoy the simple pleasures of getting up later and having someone else do the cooking.

Apart from Christmas, the fortnight in Blackpool held the greatest thrill for me as a child. Most families like mine, on modest incomes and where the breadwinner had limited time off work, had neither the money nor the opportunity to travel and see the world, and therefore spent the holidays at one of Britain's seaside resorts. Rotherham is about as far as you can get from the sea so, apart from the day trips to Scarborough, Filey and Bridlington and the school trips to the Isle of Man, I saw little of the coast. There was therefore an extraordinary feeling of excitement and anticipation when the summer holiday came around.

There was much to see and do in that bright, garish, noisy town so different from the place in which I lived.

---

stealing towels from the guests.

I recall the promenade illuminated by a million coloured lights, the huge piers stretching out into the battleship-grey ocean, the packed beach with hardly a gap between the deckchairs, pink-and-white sticky rock shot through with the name 'Blackpool'.

I can still see the seafront shops selling fish and chips, whelks, candy floss, breezy postcards, cheesy souvenirs and silly cowboy hats with suggestive slogans on the front. I can still taste the hot dogs with mustard which burnt my tongue and the greasy onions drizzled on the top; the blocks of Wall's ice cream supplied with the cone with the rectangular opening in which to put it.

Then there were the donkey rides and the Punch and Judy, the trundling open-topped trams travelling along decked out in bright lights and, of course, the Tower, rising in a lattice of metal, and Reginald Dixon playing *O, I Do Like to be Beside the Seaside* on the great organ.

The hotel was so dull I sent down for another Bible.

I can also recall the Blackpool boarding house where we spent our holidays. The Phinn family (Mum and Dad, brothers Michael and Alec, and sister Christine) stayed at Mrs Cadwallader's boarding house near Gynn Square, which always seemed to be full of Scottish people. It was a substantial three-storey terrace with, I guess, five or six bedrooms. The front room downstairs was set out with four dining tables for the guests. There were strict rules about mealtimes, use of the bathroom, about coming in 'after hours' and about keeping down the noise.

If all the year were playing holidays
To sport would be as tedious as to work.
Shakespeare

I've never taken a hotel towel,

The food was plain and very often inedible. Breakfast was always cornflakes, undercooked fried eggs swimming in fat, greasy rashers of smoked bacon and fried bread followed by cold toast. Salad was the staple meal for tea: big weeping chunks of boiled ham or thin slices of corned beef (which resembled Mrs Cadwallader's legs in colour and texture), hard-boiled eggs with blobs of salad cream on top, over-ripe tomatoes and wilting lettuce.

Her offerings on Saturday and Sunday were sometimes more substantial: tepid brown Windsor soup followed by a fleshy, boneless piece of steak with the consistency of shoe leather, accompanied by vegetables which had been boiled tasteless; or her famed Lancashire hotpot — chunks of grey meat, swollen kidneys and chopped carrots swimming in a lake of thin, greasy gravy. This would be followed by apple pie: a glutinous concoction of sour-tasting fruit beneath pale, flaccid pastry. Should we children betray the slightest dissatisfaction or leave too much on the plate, the

---

and I've got the silverware to prove it.

landlady's thin lips would purse in displeasure. We took to slyly emptying our mouths in our handkerchiefs and disposing of the evidence later down the toilet.

For Friday's dinner, being Catholics, we were served fish: chunks of lukewarm cod smothered in a sticky white sauce with sprigs of parsley sprinkled on the top and accompanied by pallid boiled potatoes and bullet-hard peas. The fish served at the fish and chip shops was scrumptious: mouth-watering, sizzling, encased in tasty batter. Once Mrs Cadwallader got her hands on a piece of fish she

There's a famous seaside place called Blackpool,
That's noted for fresh air and fun...
***The Lion and Albert*, by Marriott Edgar**

It is always a holiday for the slothful. — Latin proverb

managed to kill it again. It was as if she meant it to be a penance. One year, on the second Friday of our stay, Mrs Cadwallader apologised for not being able to get any fish.

"Oh dear," sighed Dad. "What a pity." He winked in my direction. "Don't you worry, Mrs Cadwallader, we'll get some fish and chips from the shop on the front."

Jim Thompson's recollections of his summer holiday in Blackpool as a child in the 1950s brought back further memories for me:

"It was the great sense of freedom that I recall. During the year my mother was careful not to let my brother David and me eat too many sweets or read too many comics or stay up too late, but during the holiday week all those restrictions seemed to go out of the window. We spent the days eating candyfloss and ice cream, sucking on sticky pink rock and

Many feel dejected after a holiday. — Latin proverb

eating greasy cod and chips smothered in salt and vinegar until we felt ill. We would stay all day on the beach getting sunburnt, building sandcastles, running in and out of the sea in these ridiculous knitted swimming trunks, riding on the donkeys, watching the Punch and Judy shows. When the sun went in we would invade the amusement arcades or sit outside one of the pubs with a dandelion and burdock and a bag of crisps, while Mum and Dad, sitting inside, enjoyed beverages of a more alcoholic nature. We were all as happy as sandboys on the way back to the boarding house."

When the Phinns arrived in Blackpool the first port of call was to W H Hills, the ice cream parlour on the front, where Dad would treat us to a knickerbocker glory: that tall, cone-shaped glass full of raspberry jelly, strawberries, chunks of tinned peach and different-flavoured ice creams, scattered liberally with crushed nuts and topped with a shiny glazed cherry. We would be given a long, shiny metal spoon, but try as we might we never did get that last bit of peach at the bottom of the glass.

Every morning my brother Alec and I, dressed in khaki shorts, white cotton caps and sandals, wearing cheap plastic sunglasses and with our Brownie box cameras around our necks on a string, would walk with Dad along the promenade from the boarding house to Gynn Square to get his paper. "Smell the ozone," Dad would say, breathing in deeply. If the tide was out he would sit in a deckchair on the beach to read his *Daily Express*, keeping a wary eye on the two boys as we ran into the sea.

I remember vividly the swimming trunks I wore: dark green, tight-fitting knitted affairs with a canvas belt and metal clasp which took some skill to keep on once sodden with water. There's a photo of me with my brother, arms around each other, shivering near the sea's edge. We had

hotels. — Herbert Beerbohm Tree

just emerged from the water and stood there in these heavy, sagging, uncomfortable outfits.

It was a nostalgic journey when I returned to Blackpool after half a century. On the promenade the smell of donkey manure, candyfloss and seaweed had remained and took me back to my youth. I sat for a moment on a bench and recalled a little boy dressed in khaki shorts, white cotton cap and sandals, wearing cheap plastic sunglasses and with his Brownie box camera around his neck on a string, walking hand-in-hand with his father.

A cruise director told me of the elderly woman on a tour of Bruges, staring at the magnificently ornate Church of Our Lady with its 377-foot high tower and remarking to her companion, "I wouldn't like to dust it". Alan Bennett, eat your heart out!

The best part of a holiday is not so much to be resting yourself,

My parents were great day-trippers and most weekends in summer found us — Mum and Dad, my two brothers and sister and myself — in a green Morris Oxford heading for the coast. It was always Whitby, Scarborough or Bridlington we visited. Mum would pack the box of sandwiches and fruitcake and fill the flasks, Dad would check the car — tyres, oil, water — and we children would be waiting excitedly, crammed in the back seat of the car, keen to be on our way. We left the smoke and grime of Rotherham behind us and headed for Thorne, Driffield and Market Weighton. It was usually my brother Alec who would ask first, "Are we nearly there yet?"

Whitby, with its quaint streets, picturesque quay and imposing abbey, was a favourite. One memorable Sunday my parents insisted we visit St Mary's Church, situated high on the clifftop. We were told there was a magnificent view over the harbour from the church and we could see

---

as to see all the other fellows busy working. — *The Wind in the Willows* the famous box pews and the three-decker pulpit. We were deeply unimpressed until Dad mentioned Count Dracula. It was just off the coast, he told us, where the ship bringing his remains to England was wrecked and in the graveyard he still roamed at midnight. One hundred and ninety-nine steps later, we arrived at the church but were not overly interested in the famous box pews and three-decker pulpit. We were in search of the vampire. When the vicar, a tall, thin, white-faced individual in a flowing black cape, appeared at the door of the church I was very impressed.

"Are you Count Dracula?" I asked innocently.

My red-faced parents hurried their little boy down the steps and back to the car.

Scarborough was another favourite holiday destination. I loved making sandcastles on the soft sandy beach; the donkey rides; steering the chugging, smelly little

---

A perpetual holiday is a good working

motorboats on the boating lake; listening to the music at the Spa; walking along the promenade, lips sticky with candyfloss and the sweet, pink sticks of rock which lasted for hours and hours. I loved the climb up to the castle and later, hungry from the walk, fish and chips with bread and butter and a pot of tea in the café on the front.

I remember one holiday we stood outside the entrance of the palatial Grand Hotel. We marvelled at the Gothic splendour: cast-iron balconies, corner domes with porthole windows, the red and orange terracotta, and the great Corinthian columns.

"When I win the football pools," I remember my father saying, "we will all stay there." Sadly, that never came to be.

John Thornton recalls childhood visits to Scarborough in the 1950s:

---

definition of hell. — George Bernard Shaw

"My mother was a strict Primitive Methodist (my father less so) and there were certain activities on our annual summer holiday in Scarborough which were taboo. We children were not allowed to go on the beach on the Sabbath, frequenting the amusement arcade was off limits, eating fish and chips out of a newspaper on the prom unthinkable and we were hurried past the shops selling the saucy postcards.

"I loved to read the wonderfully rude postcards with their double meanings in the captions and I would sneak back when my mother was out of sight. The brightly coloured postcards always seemed to feature massive women with great bosoms in tight, striped bathing costumes, busty blondes and small, harassed-looking, bald-headed men. One showed such a man in a skimpy pair of trunks with a small dog at his feet asking a startled woman, 'Do you like my little Willy?'

"The Punch and Judy Show fascinated me but we were

There is a French widow in every bedroom, affording

not allowed to watch it with the other children. 'Far too violent,' announced my mother. I would sneak away to watch the show and loved Mr Punch with his humped back and gigantic curved nose knocking hell out of the policeman with his truncheon, hitting the baby, clunking his wife and sorting out the crocodile. When he appeared he would be greeted by wild cheers from the children.

"My father, too, was not above sneaking away from the beady eyes of my mother. He would have a crafty half and a woodbine when he got the chance. One day I spotted him amongst the many people (mostly men) watching the bathing beauty competition. Long-legged young women in tight-fitting bathing costumes paraded at the outdoor bathing pool. 'Don't worry, Dad,' I told him with a wink as he walked me back to where my mother was sitting in a deckchair on the sands, 'I won't say anything.' He slipped me a sixpence."

---

delightful prospects. — reputedly in letter from landlord

Memories of knitted swimwear

"I doubt that today's fashion-conscious youngsters would be seen dead in some of the make-do-and-mend clothing we were forced into wearing in the decades immediately following the Second World War. Top of my list of homemade garments to avoid was a pair of knitted swimming trunks. I'm sure my mum and grandma were both very pleased with their money-saving creations as they held them aloft for inspection after hours of clickety-clicking. But that was before the trunks got wet. Mine were supposed to be held up by one of Dad's old bootlaces, but that was never going to be strong enough against the pulling power of the tide at Scarborough. Without having an extra pair of hands to carry a bucket and spade while holding your trunks up at the same time, it wasn't possible to keep your dignity on the beach. And once they became caked in wet sand you may as well have been dragging a bag of cement between your legs."

Paul Jackson

"In 1938 when I was eleven years old, Mother knitted me a bathing costume in buttercup yellow with brown stripes – I looked like a bumble bee."

Joyce Hughes

"I remember knitted swimsuits. My mother found a pattern for an adult-sized bikini, which she reproduced in black and white. As this was the early 1950s, the bottom half extended well up over her waist, and the top was similarly modest in size. The finished article looked very successful, but unfortunately this stunning little number only had the one outing as it was no match for gravity once the seawater had met it."

Diane Myhill

"On family holidays in the late 1940s, my sister and I had to wear awful saggy knitted costumes. When wet they weighed a ton and sagged even more. I remember my joy when presented with a rouched cotton costume several years later."

Miggie Bruce

Bernie Clifton, the comedian, told me that his little grandson, when on holiday with him, announced that he had been for a wee in the sea. "But it's all right, Grandad," he added, "I waited 'til the water covered my willy."

Here Ken Williams recalls a memorable visit to Yorkshire's finest seaside spa town:

"We spent quite a bit of our holiday at the swimming pool in Scarborough. My little brother Graham, aged six, was a good little swimmer and was in and out of the sea. If it was wet and windy it was off to the swimming pool. On one occasion the pool attendant came over to my mother with a

---

Twenty-four hour room service generally refers to the length of stony face, pushing my little brother before him.

'Is this your lad?' he asked Mum angrily.

'It is,' replied my mother. 'What's he done?'

'He's been peeing in the water.'

'Is that all?' said my mother. 'Lots of little boys wee in the water.'

'Not from the diving board they don't!' retorted the attendant."

Sadly for many, those seaside holidays in places like Whitby and Scarborough are things of the past. They hold little attraction any more. People now prefer a package holiday in Spain or Greece, where the climate is virtually guaranteed to be warm and the hotels cater for the influx of tourists. Characters like Mrs Cadwallader and Mrs

---

time it takes for the club sandwich to arrive. — Fran Lebowitz

Wilson are figures of the past, the Punch and Judy and the bathing beauty competitions have disappeared, regarded as politically incorrect. In those bright and sunny holidays of the past no-one seemed to grumble about the long coach journey or the traffic jams, the cold weather or the teeming

Summer was over, and in the primary school the teacher was asking the class 'What we did on our holidays'.

"We visited my grandmother who lives in Pontrhydfendigaid in Wales," said young Jake.

The teacher asked, "Good, and can you tell the class how you spell that?"

Jake replied, "My mistake. Actually, she lives in Bath."

rain, cramped boarding house or the poor-quality fare. Not so today. According to travel agents, people these days are only too ready to whinge and moan, as these comments taken from a survey by Thomas Cook and ABTA bear testimony:

"The beach was too sandy."

"On my holiday to Goa in India, I was disgusted to find that almost every restaurant served curry. I don't like spicy food at all."

A tourist at a top African game lodge overlooking a waterhole, who spotted a visibly aroused elephant, complained that the sight of this rampant beast ruined her honeymoon by making her husband feel "inadequate".

How he got into my pyjamas I'll never know. — Groucho Marx

"It's lazy of the local shopkeepers to close in the afternoons. I often needed to buy things during 'siesta' time."

"Topless sunbathing on the beach should be banned. The holiday was ruined, as my husband spent all day looking at other women."

"There are too many Spanish people in our hotel at Benidorm. The receptionist spoke Spanish. The food is Spanish. Too many foreigners now live abroad."

"My fiancé and I booked a twin-bedded room but we were placed in a double-bedded room. We now hold you responsible for the fact that I find myself pregnant. This would not have happened if you had put us in the room that we booked."

The great advantage of a hotel is that it's a

A popular vacation, particularly for the more mature holidaymaker, is the cruise. My friend Hamish Reid, who for many years was a captain with P&O Cruises, recalls a few memorable incidents, including a fight in the launderette, a tipsy clergyman who sang *The Old Rugged Cross* in the Crowsnest Bar and could not be prevailed upon to shut up until he had sung the whole five verses, the concert pianist who missed the ship in Vigo, and the objectionable Lottery winner who was put off in Gibraltar with all his rowdy guests. Hamish was once asked by a passenger if the crew slept on board. He was tempted to reply, "Oh no, we fly them in by helicopter each morning."

This day, for me a true holiday, shall banish gloomy cares.
Horace

---

refuge from home life. — George Bernard Shaw

Hamish recalls one conversation on board ship:

Passenger: Has the ten-thirty tender gone?

Captain: Yes, it has, madam.

Passenger: What time did it go?

Captain: At ten thirty.

Passenger: When is the next one?

Captain: In ten minutes.

Passenger: When we're ashore, where does it pick us up?

Captain: On the jetty.

Passenger: Which end of the jetty does it go from?

Captain: The part that is in the water, madam.

A good holiday is one spent among people whose notions of time are vaguer than yours.
J B Priestley

I suppose we all have recollections of our earlier holidays,

Overheard on the cruise ship *Aurora*, which had to return to port with engine trouble:

Wife: Shurrup complaining.

Husband: We're supposed to be on the world cruise and we're stuck here in Southampton staring at the gasworks.

Wife: You've done nothing but complain since we got on the boat.

Husband: It's a ship.

Wife: Oh, hark at Admiral Nelson. Since when have you been an expert on boats and ships? You get sick on a boating lake.

Husband: Some holiday this.

Wife: I'm sick to death of hearing you moaning. You'd have something to complain about if we were in the middle of the ocean and were swept away on a satsuma.

Summer holidays, for those of us born before the mid-1960s when foreign travel took over, usually consisted of a short trip to the coast or countryside by train or charabanc. No matter how cheap or simple the holiday, memories linger long. After all, the sun always shone, and Dad was fun instead of grumpy and Mum gave us everything we asked for … okay, perhaps not, but at least the holidays meant no school for six weeks for children and a week off work for parents.

The traditional seaside boarding house was popular with my family — though we were locked out of the 'digs' between 11am and 4pm, no matter what the weather was like.

The journey was part of the holiday for many people, even though most did not travel very far. I loved going away by steam train, being in charge of my own little evacuee-style suitcase.

Looking back at old photos of family holidays, I chuckle at what parents and grandparents wore on the beach. One of my granddads can be seen in a deckchair wearing his best shoes, a suit, waistcoat, shirt and tie — his only concession to summer being the exchange of his flat cap for a straw boater.

Paul Jackson

In the 1950s I knew an elderly farmer who embarked on the only holiday of his long lifetime — a trip to the Isle of Man. He stood, in best suit and polished boots, waiting for my father to drive him to the railway station. "Where is your suitcase?" asked my father. The old man produced a spare shirt collar from his pocket. "Nay, lad," he said. "I'm only going for the week."

John Mellin

The play's the thing

The theatre

It is a truism, of course, that what makes one person happy does not necessarily make another person happy. The athlete standing proudly on the podium at the Olympic Games with a gold medal draped around his or her neck, the sportsperson scoring that vital goal in the last minute of a crucial game, the student opening the envelope to learn the examinations have been passed with flying colours — all, of course, feel on cloud nine. Hearing from the doctor that the illness is not as serious as was first thought, seeing your child in the nativity play, winning the Lottery — there are so many occasions when one is filled with a great feeling of elation.

I saw the play under adverse conditions.

For me, I am never happier than when I sit in a theatre and am taken into another world, hearing the words of the playwright lifted from the page, and sharing laughter and sometimes tears with others in the audience.

Until Mr Williams, my former headmaster at secondary school, stopped me in the corridor one day when I was studying for my O-Levels and gave me two tickets to see Sheridan's comic masterpiece *The Rivals*, my experience of theatre had been limited to the end-of-the-pier shows at Blackpool and the Christmas pantomime. I had never seen any classic drama, and as I watched *The Rivals* on that memorable Saturday evening I was engrossed.

Once hooked, I would try to see as many productions as I could. I paid for the tickets by supplementing my pocket money, by getting a paper round and by digging Mr Williams' garden, and I became a regular member of the audience at Rotherham Civic, Sheffield Playhouse, Doncaster Civic and the Sheffield Lyceum.

The curtain was up. — Robert Benchley

Miss Wainwright, my A-Level English teacher, took the class to see a production of *King Lear* at Rotherham Civic Theatre. The acting was wooden and the costumes bizarre, but the beauty and poignancy of the language had come through. King Lear, confused and deranged, entered with his dead daughter in his arms, crying to the heavens:

"Howl, howl, howl, howl! O, you are men of stones:
Had I your tongues and eyes, I'd use them so
That heaven's vault should crack. She's gone forever.
I know when one is dead and when one lives.
She's dead as earth."

Miss Wainwright — sitting one away from me in the row — began to dab her eyes with her lace handkerchief.

"I hear they are making Richard III into a musical. It's going to be called, I Have a Hunch, I'm Going to be King."

The owner of the camping shop clearly had a good knowledge of the famous lines from *Richard III*:

"Now is the winter of our discontent
Made glorious summer by this sun of York."

At Christmas he displayed a large announcement in his shop window:

"Now it is Winter, it's our Discount Tents."

Theatres are curious places, magician's trick-boxes where the golden memories of dramatic triumphs linger like nostalgic ghosts, and where the unexplainable, the fantastic, the tragic, the comic and the absurd are routine occurrences on and off the stage.

E A Bucchianeri

I thought I'd begin by reciting a sonnet by Shakespeare but then

Just before he died, Laurence Olivier was asked by an eager reporter if acting was "as much fun as it used to be". Lord Olivier slowly eyed him up and down and then replied, "Young man, I am now eighty years old. Nothing is as much fun as it used to be!"

At a party to celebrate the end of a successful season in Stratford upon Avon, an actor went up to the artistic director Sir Trevor Nunn, and they began to chat about the programme he had scheduled for the following year. Then the actor got rather serious, and asked Nunn's opinion on who he thought had really written the plays of Shakespeare — was it the Bard himself, or Francis Bacon? Nunn thought for a moment, and said with a twinkle in his eye that he fervently hoped that it was the former, because "I don't want to be the director of the Royal Bacon Company".

I thought why should I? He never reads any of mine. — Spike Milligan

Performing Shakespeare to a theatre full of schoolchildren must be an actor's worst nightmare. In one production of *Macbeth* things went well until the harrowing scene when the son of Macduff is stabbed to death. Lady Macduff, holding her child, talked to him soothingly centre stage, unaware of the two murderers creeping from the shadows. As they approached, knives in hands, there came a voice from the audience, "Behind you!"

Graham Allen, the distinguished former drama adviser for Wakefield, reminded me of this episode when a young actor settled a score on stage. I guess this is an apocryphal account (my colleague was a great storyteller and consummate actor), but it is well worth repeating.

Graham chaired a panel which awarded grants for sixth-form students to attend music and drama colleges. One particular young man was very talented — but also

---

The play was a great success,

extremely arrogant — and had applied to RADA, the prestigious drama college. After a bravura performance as Hamlet for his audition, the young man won his award and the inspector was asked by the boy's headmaster if he would like to see the young man in action playing the lead in the school's production of *Macbeth*. The future star of the London stage was indeed very convincing as the Scottish tyrant and dominated the scenes, dwarfing all the other actors with his outstanding performance.

Musical comedy is the Irish stew of drama. Anything may be put into it, with the certainty that it will improve the general effect.
P G Wodehouse

On the first night, the eleven-year-old boy playing the part of Seyton, an officer attending Macbeth, a rather insignificant part compared to others in the play, made his entrance to inform Macbeth of the Queen's demise. With bowed head and in a faltering voice the boy delivered his one line, "The Queen, my Lord, is dead", and exited stage left. Macbeth then launches into his memorable soliloquy:

"She should have died hereafter;
There would have been a time for such a word.
Tomorrow and tomorrow and tomorrow
Creeps in this petty pace from day to day,
To the last syllable of recorded time..."

At the second night's performance, Seyton's relatives were in the audience — in fact the first two rows were crammed with parents, siblings, uncles, aunts, cousins and neighbours. They waited patiently for the entrance of the boy. When the young actor entered the stage to deliver his

---

one line there was an audible in-drawing of breath from the assorted relations and friends, and the whispered voice of a proud mother from the front row could be heard announcing "That's our Wayne". Seeing his adoring fans, the boy decided to embellish his part a little and, throwing his arms in the air, he wailed, "The Queen, my Lord, is dead! She's dead! She's dead! She's dead!" In one final harrowing shout he announced as he beat his breast, "She's deeeeaaaaad!" He then left the stage to thunderous applause from the front two rows.

The future star of RADA was not at all pleased when he found the boy in the dressing room later. There were histrionics on a grand scale. "Just say your line and get off the stage!" he ordered, before strutting off to remove his make-up.

On the last night of the production young Seyton, still smarting from the reprimand, entered the stage to deliver

---

how did you enjoy the play?" (apocryphal)

his line. Macbeth prepared himself for his powerful soliloquy but was rather lost for words when the boy announced, "The Queen, my Lord, is making a remarkable recovery".

The school inspectors had been invited to see the school production of *Anne of Green Gables*. The lead part of Anne, played by a plump, red-faced girl with protuberant blue eyes, was undertaken with great enthusiasm and confidence. Dressed in a bright blue-and-yellow gingham smock and sporting huge bunches of hair tied in red ribbons, she dominated the stage. She declaimed her lines in a dreadful mock-American drawl at the rate of a Gatling gun and had the irritating habit of waving her hands in front of her as if conducting some imaginary orchestra.

The play came to an end.

Leaving the school hall, one inspector caught sight of the

Shakespeare is fantastic. And to think

pale, slight girl who had delivered the play's opening lines.

"You were excellent," he told her.

"I only had a few lines," replied the child, smiling coyly.

"Ah," the important visitor said, "but you were the first person to speak and it was you who set the scene. We heard every word clearly and if I had an Oscar to award — you know, the prizes that very famous actors and actresses sometimes get — well, I would give it to you."

"That was a lovely thing to say," said his colleague.

"She deserved an Oscar," said the inspector. "Anyone who could go on to the stage, before all the other actors, beneath all those bright lights, in front of a hundred people and deliver such ridiculous lines without making one mistake, deserves an Oscar."

"What did she say?" asked his colleague. "I can't remember."

"'Is Farmer Hart's farm far from here?'," he replied.

---

he wrote it all with a feather! — Sam Goldwyn

Comments by theatregoers:

A woman, on hearing Macbeth say "Tomorrow and tomorrow and tomorrow", remarked to her companion, "So that'll be Monday then."

"It was all right but there were too many words." (On *Hamlet*)

"They only did half of it." (On *Henry IV, Part I*)

"I didn't think there would be so many cats in it." (On *Cats*)

"It's not called *Henry Vee*. Those are Roman numerals. It's pronounced *Henry Five*." (On *Henry V*)

"He won't come, you know, because his name's not in the programme." (On *Waiting for Godot*)

"It was all right if you like laughing." (On *Spamalot*)

"Is the dress circle near the stalls?"

"I want to take my grandchildren. It's not too violent, is it?" (On *The Railway Children*)

Man to woman who was speaking loudly behind him during a theatre performance: "I'm afraid I didn't quite catch what you were saying because of all the noise on stage."

Woman to man sitting in the seat behind her at the theatre: "Would you mind not putting your programme in my hair?" Man to woman: "Well, would you mind not putting your hair in my programme?"

In a particularly poor stage production of *Anne Frank*'s *Diary*, in the last act the Gestapo arrived to arrest the family. As two sinister figures appeared on stage, someone in the audience shouted, "They're in the attic!"

The production of *Hamlet* was particularly violent in the final act. Laertes stabbed Hamlet, Hamlet stabbed Laertes, Gertrude drank from the poisoned chalice, screamed and collapsed, writhing and frothing at the mouth. This was closely followed by Hamlet stabbing and throttling Claudius, who fell from his throne covered in blood and dropped down dead. Hamlet then clutched his throat and expired. There was a stunned hush in the theatre. A woman in the audience was heard to remark to her companion: "And I only hope the dog hasn't been sick in the car."

I daren't tell my mother I'm starring in *The Vagina Monologues*. I've told her it's called *The Geneva Monologues*, and it's about women in banking.
Maureen Lipman

Don't clap too hard — it's a very old building. — John Osborne

Young Actor: Did Hamlet actually sleep with Ophelia?
Old Actor: I don't know about the West End, laddie, but we always did on tour.

In the penultimate act of the murder-mystery drama, the deceived husband enters the stage to discover his wife in the arms of his best friend.

"So it is you, Rupert!" he snarls. "The man my wife has been seeing."

He then produces a pistol from his pocket and shoots his wife's lover as the curtain falls.

Celebrated Shakespearean actor Edmund Kean's stage direction to any new actor he worked with: "Stand upstage of me and do your worst."

Said Hamlet to Ophelia, "I'll draw a sketch of thee; what kind

The play had been performed for months, and the actor playing the husband had become rather blasé about things and timed his arrival on stage with only seconds to spare. On one night he forgot to put the gun in his pocket. He entered the stage.

"So it is you, Rupert!" he snarled. "The man my wife has been seeing."

He reached into his pocket but there was no gun.

Thinking on his feet, he rushed across the stage and kicked the wife's lover on the shin. "Poison boots!" he cried.

An actor gets a call from his agent. "I've got a job for you. It's only a one-liner but could lead to greater things."

"What's the line?" the actor asks.

"'Hark, I hear the cannons roar'," the agent tells him. "The audition is next Wednesday."

The actor goes to the audition.

---

of pencil shall I use? 2B or not 2B?" — Spike Milligan

"All you have to say is, 'Hark, I hear the cannons roar'," explains the director.

The actor enters and declaims loudly and with feeling, "Hark, I hear the cannons roar."

"Excellent," says the director.

On the first night the actor is held up in traffic. He finally gets to the theatre minutes before the start of the performance. "Hark, I hear the cannons roar. Hark, I hear the cannons roar," he keeps repeating. He is stopped at the stage door.

"Who are you?" asks the doorman.

"I'm 'Hark, I hear the cannons roar'," the actor tells him.

"You're late. Quick, get to make-up," says the doorman.

"Who are you?" asks the woman in make-up

"I'm 'Hark, I hear the cannons roar'," the actor tells her.

She quickly applies the make-up. "You had better change into your costume and get down to the stage. It's your entrance in a couple of minutes."

Last time I acted, my name was so low on the programme

So the actor changes and dashes down to the stage. "'Hark, I hear the cannons roar. Hark, I hear the cannons roar'," he keeps repeating.

"Who are you?" asks the stage manager.

"I'm 'Hark, I hear the cannons roar'," the actor tells him.

"Thank goodness," says the stage manager, "you are just in time. This is your cue."

So the actor walks on to the stage. Suddenly there is an almighty bang behind him.

"What the hell was *that*?" he cries.

Brush up your Shakespeare
Start quoting him now.
Brush up your Shakespeare
And the women you will wow.
Cole Porter

I was getting orders for the printing. — Frank Carson

Many happy returns!
Birthdays

Looking back to my childhood, one of the happiest times in my life was the day of my birthday. I guess it is for most of us.

It was the time when I was the very centre of everyone's attention, made a fuss of, bought presents and had a party. Coming down for breakfast on my birthday I would find a specially made cake, decorated with my name and studded with the same number of candles as my age. I wasn't allowed to touch it. There would be presents and, later, a party for a few of my friends.

My birthday tea, as my mother called it, was a low-key affair in those days. Just two or three pals would be invited

---

He always remembers his wife's birthday;

to the house for a few sandwiches, a bun or two and a piece of cake. My father would make himself scarce. We would amuse ourselves with my new presents for a while, play a game or two, and then the candles on the cake would be lit and I would attempt to blow them out in one breath. Then I would make a wish (kept secret, of course, or it wouldn't come true) and everyone would sing *Happy Birthday to You*.

The first fact about the celebration of a birthday is that it is a way of affirming defiantly, and even flamboyantly, that it is a good thing to be alive.
G K Chesterton

---

it's the day after she reminds him of it.

The child's birthday party can be a delightful, happy occasion and have some very pleasing and unexpected outcomes, as Tricia Norman knows:

"I am the first to admit that I am not the world's best cook but I decided, rather than buy the food for my daughter's tenth birthday party, I would have a go at making the food myself. I baked a cake which didn't quite turn out as I had hoped. It was lumpy and looked dry and my attempts at icing the top made it look like the aftermath of an avalanche. Bits kept falling off. The buns were misshapen and looked burnt. Even the sandwiches looked sad. It was too late to get to the shops so the food I had prepared would have to do. My husband viewed my efforts with an expressionless face. I asked him to sample one of the buns and tell me what he thought. He took a small bite. When he didn't say anything I asked if it tasted all right.

I grew up so poor I didn't celebrate my

'Well, it's different, I'll give you that,' he told me.

'If I baked some of these for the church summer fair, what do you think I'd get for them?' I asked. He thought for a moment and then replied, 'I reckon about five years'.

You can imagine how delighted I was when all I had cooked disappeared in no time at the party, and how smug I felt when one little girl told me the buns were 'yummy' and the cake was 'scrumptious'."

But a child's birthday party can also turn into something of a nightmare...

"With regard to my son's birthday parties, I learnt the hard way. I now abandon the party at home for a horde of noisy children, and take just a few of his friends to the cinema and for a burger. The party which very nearly gave me a nervous breakdown was when my son was eight.

---

eighteenth birthday until I was twenty-three.

The ten little boys were so hyped up they wouldn't sit down or play any games and ran around like dervishes, knocking over ornaments and making a real racket. I had prepared a lovely spread of sandwiches, sausage rolls, mini pork pies, sausages on toothpicks, cheese fingers and a selection of cakes and buns. The children swooped on the food like starving gannets, leaving anything that looked vaguely savoury and attacking the sweet stuff. Of course, I might have predicted one of them would be sick. He vomited over the carpet, the sofa, the coffee table, the electric fire and then, with a great final effort, on me."

Gill Smith

A friend never defends a husband who gets his wife an electric skillet for her birthday.
Erma Bombeck

Will You Come to My Party?

Will you come to my party?
Oh, please say that you will come.
There'll be lots to eat and lots to drink.
It really will be fun.

The philosopher observed: "I'll think about it."
The musician trilled: "Sounds good to me."
The psychiatrist thought it a mad idea.
The butler said: "I'll wait and see."
The psychologist replied that she'd bear it in mind.
The meteorologist said: "Fine."
The greengrocer remarked that he'd weigh things up.
The horologist would if he had the time.
The insomniac sighed she'd sleep on it.
"I'm sorry," the penitent said.
The optician concluded: "It looks all right."

My wife hasn't had a birthday for four years.

The librarian said: "Take it as read."
The cardiologist hadn't the heart to refuse.
The wrangler whooped: "Yippee!"
The inventor declared: "I can make it, all right."
The escapologist said: "If I'm free."
The fisherman told me he'd drop me a line.
The rugby player promised he'd try.
The campanologist said he'd give me a ring.
The examiner asked me: "Why?"
The parachutist said that he might drop in.
The informer that he would let me know.
"I'd love to come," the fiancé cried.
The killjoy answered: "No!"
The wrestler growled he would put it on hold.
The rambler said: "I'm on my way."
"Oh, I'll be there," the naturist said.
"I've nothing on that day."

"Which state were you born in?" "The nude".

So glad you could make it!
Do come in...

For my wife's sixtieth birthday I organised a surprise party. With great secrecy I invited family and friends to an evening celebration at a country house hotel. I told our four children to dissemble and convince their mother they were not able to make her birthday that year.

Richard telephoned from London. "Sorry Mum, I can't be with you. I'm so busy at work."

Matthew emailed from Japan. "I would have loved to be there, Mum, but can't manage to get a flight. Hope you understand."

Dominic telephoned from China. ”I'm a bit strapped for cash, so sadly won't be home for your birthday. Sorry Mum."

Elizabeth got in touch from Newcastle. "I have a really important meeting at work. Can't miss it I'm afraid. Have a lovely birthday, Mum."

Although clearly upset that none of our children would

My wife is very economical. She only used

be with her on the special day, Christine was philosophical.

"Well, it can't be helped," she sighed.

The morning of her birthday the telephone rang.

"It's Dominic," came the crackly voice down the line. "It's a bad connection here in China. Hope you can hear me. I just wanted to wish you a happy birthday."

The doorbell rang.

"Just a moment," said Christine, "there's someone at the front door."

She opened the door to find Dominic with his mobile phone at his ear, and with his brothers and sister smiling behind him.

"Surprise!" they shouted in unison.

Christine's reaction was unexpected. She burst into tears.

---

twenty-six candles on her fortieth birthday cake.

Letter to parents from the headteacher: "On the afternoon of Saturday the 24th June we will be celebrating the one hundredth birthday of the opening of our school. There will be amusement stalls, a brass band, a bouncy castle and many other activities so do come along with your children to celebrate this very special occasion. At three o'clock there will be a surprise appearance of Peppa Pig. This will be followed by a hog roast."

At a rather posh birthday reception in the 1930s, a guest recognised a very elegant woman speaking to the hostess. He knew the face but could not recall the name. He was certain he had seen her before and tried to remember where. When he got the opportunity he went over to speak to her.

The older you get, the more you need to keep a

"Good evening," he said.
"Good evening," she replied.
"And how are you these days?"
"I'm very well, thank you."
"And how is your husband keeping?"
"He's very well too."
"And tell me, what is he doing these days?"
"Oh, he's still king," replied Queen Mary.

Franklin Adams, an American journalist and writer of light funny poems, once tested Beatrice Kaufman by asking her whose birthday it was that day.

"Yours?" she guessed.

"No, but you are getting warm," said Adams. "It's Shakespeare's."

---

fire extinguisher close to the cake. — Greg Tamblyn

"I think it's wonderful you could all be here for the forty-third anniversary of my thirty-ninth birthday. We decided not to light the candles this year – we were afraid Pan Am would mistake it for a runway."

Bob Hope, on his eighty-second birthday

Great Aunt Edna had reached her one hundredth birthday. All the family gathered to celebrate this momentous event. The other residents of the care home were asked to join us in the lounge for a glass of champagne. Alex, the care assistant, a delightful young Polish man with a very pronounced foreign accent, explained that sadly Edna would probably not recognise anyone for she was in the later stages of Alzheimer's.

"She is lovely old lady," he said, "but she remembers very little."

At the reception there was just one male resident — a tall, stern-faced, ex-grammar school headmaster, who was telling those who would listen about what the different sizes of champagne bottle were called. He stopped when he heard Alex ask Great Aunt Edna if she recognised any of the guests. She smiled but said nothing.

"Sometimes she even forgets her own name," said the care assistant. "It is so sad."

He looked at my aunt and took her hand in his. "Vas is your name?" Alex asked.

"Don't tell him, Pike!" barked the ex-headmaster.

Dennis Mason

Grandmother: When is your birthday?
Granddaughter: The fifth of March.
Grandmother: What year?
Granddaughter, sighing: Every year, Gran.

---

you don't have to get old. — George Burns

My brother's seventieth birthday party was held in the south of France, where he has a house. It was a memorable occasion — but not for the best of reasons.

The short taxi ride from the airport in Nice put me in a grumpy frame of mind for a start.

"Thirty euro, monsieur," said the taxi driver.

"How much?!" I cried.

The taxi driver shrugged. "You are in France, monsieur."

The evening before the party, the family went for a meal in a restaurant in Vence. I glanced down the menu and

Middle age is when your old classmates are so grey and wrinkled and bald they don't recognise you.
Bennet Cerf

when I saw the prices I gave the Yorkshireman's war-cry again: "How much?!"

I ordered a steak, telling the waiter I would like it well done.

"In France, monsieur," he told me, "we never cook a steak well done."

"Well, I am the customer and in Yorkshire that is how we like it," I told him.

"To over-cook a steak will ruin the flavour," he persisted. "In France we 'ave our steaks rare."

"I don't," I replied. "I'd like it well done."

He returned after some time and presented me with a black and burnt offering which sat in the middle of the plate.

"*Bon appétit*," he said with a smug expression.

"Just as I like it," I said, which wiped the smile off his face.

The number one cause of death is too many birthdays.

My brother insisted that no one should bring a present but suggested we might like to bring a dessert. In the patisserie a rather tasty-looking flan with glazed fruit on the top caught my eye.

"I would like the fruit flan, please," I told the shopkeeper.

"Monsieur," she said, "It ees not a fruit flan. It is a *tarte amandine aux poires*."

"In Yorkshire it's a fruit flan," I told her, taking out my wallet.

"That will be thirty euro," she said.

"*Combien*?!" I exclaimed.

As I carried the extortionately priced confection in a cardboard box through the streets of Vence, a dog shot out in front of me, and the pear tart flew out of my hands and ended up in the gutter.

"Thirty euro," I sighed. "Thirty euro."

I could have wept.

The seven ages of man: spills, drills, thrills,

"You know you're old when by the time the last candle is lit on your birthday cake, the first one has burnt out."

Of course no birthday would be the same without the presents. Every birthday my father bought me a book. These formed a precious collection, my own little library, and I have them still. As I look up from my desk now I see a shelf full of those adventure stories my father bought for me when I was a child: *Thomas the Tank Engine*, Enid Blyton, Biggles, Anthony Hope's swashbuckling *The Prisoner of Zenda* and *Rupert of Hentzau*, John Buchan's gripping *The Thirty Nine Steps*, Chesterton's thrilling *The Man Who Was Thursday*, Edgar Rice Burroughs' *Tarzan of the Apes*, Erskine Childers' masterpiece *The Riddle of the Sands*, and of course *Treasure Island*. My father would write a small message or adage in the front.

---

bills, ills, pills and wills. — Richard J Needham

With six of us living in the house, there was little space to keep anything and I would complain that I never had anywhere to put my books. That changed on my eleventh birthday. I woke up that day to discover a shed at the bottom of the garden. Mum had taken me to visit my grandmother the day before (when my father erected the shed and I was out of the way). It was dark when we returned home so I never saw it until the next morning. My father had put a piece of carpet on the floor, nailed a plank of wood to the inside to act as my bookshelf, and placed an old armchair in the middle and a small table to the side. It

"I'm not saying she's old, but when I tried to count the candles on her birthday cake I was driven back by the heat."

The secret of staying young and happy is to

was the best present I ever received, and in the summer months I would spend many a happy hour in my sanctuary reading until the light began to fade and my father would call me in for tea.

"It's my wife's birthday tomorrow. Last week I asked her what she wanted as a present. 'Oh, I don't know,' she said. 'Just give me something with diamonds.' I'm giving her a pack of playing cards."

I thought I would buy my wife something very special for her sixtieth birthday. She had always wanted a sports car, so I splashed out and bought her a small, bright green Toyota MR2. On the morning of her birthday, I parked the car on the drive and tied a pink ribbon around the bonnet. She was ecstatic and was keen to take the car for spin. I told

---

live honestly, eat slowly, and lie about your age.

her to take care. Off she went, arriving back home ten minutes later looking rather sheepish.

"So how do you like the car?" I asked.

"It's wonderful, darling," she replied. Then there was a pause. "And you'll be pleased to know that the airbag works."

"You'll enjoy being sixty," the eighty-five-year-old said to his son. "You can officially start using your back and memory as excuses to get out of anything you don't want to do."

A couple had not been getting along for years, so the husband thinks that he will buy his wife a cemetery plot for her birthday.

The following year, her birthday comes around again but this time he doesn't get her anything.

"Why didn't you get me a birthday present?" she asked him.

"You didn't use what I got you last year!" he replied.

Son: You know, Dad, I have my eye on that bike for my birthday.

Father: Well just keep your eye on it because you'll not get your bottom on it.

(This account is not true of course, but it brought a smile to my lips.)

A family had twin boys whose only resemblance to each other was their looks. If one felt it was too hot, the other thought it was too cold. If one said the television was

---

to being under it. — Bruce Lansky

too loud, the other claimed the volume needed to be turned up. Opposite in every way, one was an eternal optimist, the other a doom-and-gloom pessimist. Just to see what would happen, on the twins' birthday their father loaded the pessimist's room with every imaginable toy and game. The optimist's room he loaded with horse manure. That night the father passed by the pessimist's room and found him sitting amid his new gifts crying bitterly.

"Why are you crying?" the father asked.

"Because my friends will be jealous, I'll have to read all these instructions before I can do anything with this stuff,

One little nine-year-old budding psychologist advised his friend, "If you want a hamster for your birthday, ask for a dog."

I've got everything I had twenty years ago,

I'll constantly need batteries, and my toys will eventually get broken," answered the pessimist twin.

Passing the optimist twin's room, the father found him dancing for joy in the pile of manure.

"What are you so happy about?" he asked.

The optimist twin replied, "There's got to be a pony in here somewhere!"

A mother decided that her ten-year-old daughter should get something practical for her birthday, so she opened a savings account for her. At the bank the assistant manager asked the girl to fill out the application form. When she came to the space to enter the name of her previous bank, she wrote 'Piggy'.

---

except now it's all lower. — Gypsy Rose Lee

Glad tidings

Christmas

Like most children, when I was young I loved Christmas more than any other occasion in the year. It was so much more to me than just the presents and the delicious food. Christmas was one of the happiest, most magical of times.

I loved the visits into Rotherham just before the festive season when the shop windows were ablaze with colour and stacked with Christmas goods, when coloured lights stretched along the high street to brighten up the otherwise dark and solid industrial Yorkshire town, when carol singers sang and the Salvation Army band played carols in All Saints' Square, with the great medieval sandstone church towering above. It was a time of year when people would seem friendlier somehow. Christmas was even more special when a light dusting of snow covered pavements and rooftops, making the dark town seem so much cleaner and brighter. I loved it when the air became so icy it burnt your cheeks and your exhaled breath came in great clouds.

At home we would make decorations (hoops of coloured cardboard fastened together to form a chain) to drape across the room, get the old imitation Christmas tree from

Christmas begins about 1st December with an office party and ends when you finally realise what you spent, around 15th April of the next year.
P J O'Rourke

---

except two. — W C Fields (advert in *Variety*)

the loft and erect it in the front room to be decorated with coloured balls, little wooden figures and tinsel. The crib with the small plaster nativity figures was given pride of place on the mantelpiece and the crucifix on the wall was taken down until the New Year.

Christmas morning I would wake up to see the bulging pillow case at the bottom of the bed. There would be a couple of tangerines and a string bag of assorted nuts,

Would that Christmas lasted the whole year through (as it ought) and that the prejudices and passions which deform our better nature were never called into action among those to whom they should ever be strangers.
Charles Dickens

Xmas makes it sound like a skin complaint. — Audrey

chocolate coins encased in gold and silver tinfoil, a box of rose-scented Turkish delights covered in powdery icing sugar, a Cadbury's selection box, a tin of McGowan's toffees, glistening dates in a strangely shaped wooden box with three camels against an orange sky on the front. There would always be a *Beano* or *Dandy* annual and one special present. One year it was a rectangular tin of watercolour paints and two camel-hair brushes, another year a collection of lead soldiers and a grey-painted plywood fort made by my father. At eleven I received roller skates and at fifteen an Olivetti portable typewriter in a pale blue case. And there was always a book, which I added to my precious collection, my own little library, and I have them still.

The excitement and anticipation of Christmas never, ever waned for me when I was young — and never does to this day.

Fforbes-Hamilton (Penelope Keith) in *To the Manor Born*

"As a child I got really excited when Dad gave the okay for us to get the Christmas decorations down from the loft. This was a memorable family time, and most importantly for me it meant the big day was not far off and perhaps this year that new bike I wanted would arrive. As with most youngsters, Christmas was a happy time for me. Here in the countryside it was very much a 'do-it-yourself' time when we would head out into the nearby woods to collect material for yule logs, find a suitable Christmas tree, seek out holly, ivy, mistletoe, cones and berries — and anything else to decorate the house."

Paul Jackson

We were so poor that we couldn't afford a turkey — we gave the budgie chest expanders.
Les Dawson

I'm walking backwards for Christmas. — Spike Milligan

One Christmas (I must have been about fifteen at the time), my mother bought me a dark brown corduroy jacket from W Muntus, Outfitters, of Rotherham. It was a horribly thick, heavy garment with wide lapels, velvety ribs and a string of brass buttons on the cuffs. It was the sort of jacket old men wore. I hated it at first sight and told my mother so. She had a pale, hurt look on her face, as if she couldn't believe what she had heard. I had wanted a tight-fitting suit like the ones the Beatles wore and a black turtleneck jumper and I had been given this shapeless, old-fashioned jacket the colour of dog dirt. I wouldn't even try it on. There was no way I was going be seen wearing this monstrosity and I stomped off upstairs.

I emerged when Christmas dinner was on the table but sat in simmering silence and picked at the turkey. I felt everyone in the family was against me for being so ungrateful. No one spoke to me, which made it even worse.

In the school nativity play, I was always

My father took me aside later in the day and told me how disappointed he was in me, how I had upset my mother, and how I should apologise and accept the coat with good grace. But I wouldn't and sat for the rest of the day in the front room, silent and morose, and listening as the rest of the family enjoyed themselves next door. Of course, sulking is the last refuge of the powerless and gets you nowhere, but I stubbornly stayed in the front room and was ignored. It was a long and dispiriting Christmas Day.

I never did apologise, and the coat, which I guess was returned to the shop, was not mentioned again. Needless to say I never got the suit like the one the Beatles wore or the black turtleneck jumper.

My mother-in-law has come around to our house at Christmas seven years running. This year we're having a change. We're going to let her in.
Les Dawson

---

picked to play Bethlehem. — Jo Brand

"I have always thought that the innocence of young children is wonderfully illustrated at Christmas when the infant nativity takes place," Mr Pendlebury told the staff.

The vicar was sitting in the staffroom two weeks before the school broke up for the Christmas holidays. He was visiting the school to take the assembly and staying to watch the rehearsal for the play which was to be performed at St Mary's the following Friday afternoon.

"Small children acting out one of the greatest stories of all time capture the very essence of this very special time of year," he continued, speaking as if he was declaiming from his pulpit. He sighed. "To see Mary, cradling a large doll representing Baby Jesus, never fails to bring a tear to my eye and Joseph, wide-eyed and innocent-faced, in a tartan dressing gown and a thick multi-coloured towel over his head, always occasions a sympathetic smile."

"Well, I can't say that the nativity play has that effect on

me, Mr Pendlebury," said Miss Tranter. "I'm afraid I have little patience with infants. They are notoriously unpredictable and unmanageable. You can never foresee what might happen once they are in front of an audience. They fidget and shuffle, twiddle their hair, scratch and pick their noses and once they catch sight of their parents and grandparents they start waving and blowing kisses and forgetting their lines. I just hope that this time we don't have a repetition of last year's fiasco."

"Excuse me, Joyce, it was not a fiasco," said Mrs Golightly, feeling peeved by the unfavourable comment. She was the teacher who produced the nativity play each Christmas, and it took her a deal of hard work and effort. "The play was very well received and I think one has to expect a few mishaps where young children are concerned."

"Oh really, Bertha," said her colleague, "it was more than a few mishaps."

Christmas is a dangerous time. Seven people die each year

"I must admit," said the vicar, recalling last year's nativity play, "there were a few unforeseen and unfortunate incidents. I am sure that this year there will be no misadventures."

"I hardly think a few hiccups could be described as 'misadventures', Mr Pendlebury," retorted Mrs Golightly, getting increasingly wounded by the criticisms. "I thought the children did very well, all things considered."

At the nativity play performed in the church the year before, there had indeed been a few unforeseen and unfortunate incidents. The boy playing Joseph, a plump, pale-faced child with a crop of wild ginger hair, had been wearing a long, brown poncho, which had been clearly too big for a small child. As he had made his entrance he had trodden on the bottom of the costume, tripped, fallen and knocked over the manger. He had then used a word that Joseph would have never uttered. Later, when the play seemed to be going well, an angry little angel in a silk gown

---

believing Christmas decorations are chocolate. — Alan Marks

and tinsel halo, who had been masked by another infant, had shouted off stage, "Can you tell the palm tree to shift, Mrs Golightly? He's blocking my view and I can't see my nana."

"And I hope this year we are not having the appearance of the Little Drummer Boy," said Miss Tranter. "He wouldn't shut up, banging that wretched tin drum."

The over-enthusiastic little boy, dressed in a soldier outfit and taking on the part of the Little Drummer Boy, had proceeded to bang the metal drum around his neck loudly and with gusto. The infant playing Mary, an angelic-looking child with a rosy prettiness, one could see was getting increasingly annoyed. Finally her face had changed to a sort of pent-up fury. She had placed Baby Jesus carefully back in the manger (a large, pink doll with frizzy hair) and had shouted at the boy, "Will you shurrup, Darren! I'm trying to gerrim off to sleep. You're doin' mi 'ead in!"

"And if I were you, Bertha," suggested Miss Tranter, "I

A good life is a collection of happy moments. — Denis Waitley would tell the parents of the Three Wise Men not to go overboard on their children's costumes this year. I mean, it's not a contest to see who the best-dressed king is."

The parents of the children playing the Magi had indeed gone to town on the costumes. The three little boys had entered the stage in regal splendour, holding their precious gifts. The first king had a huge silver turban perched on his head and a purple cloak (a velvet curtain) embellished with sequins draped around him. The second king had worn a headdress of coloured feathers, white gloves and a scarlet pashmina. King number three had sported a most impressive bejewelled cardboard crown. The jewels in his crown were in fact coloured wine gums which had been glued on to look like rubies and emeralds and they had shone brilliantly under the lights.

As the play had progressed, the third king had begun to get rather bored and had started yawning and scratching

---

A day without laughter is a wasted day. — Charlie Chaplin

and stretching. Then he had proceeded to detach the wine gums one by one from his crown, pop them in his mouth and chew them vigorously. The other two kings had watched him with interest. Finally the second king had leaned over and said in a loud stage whisper, "Give us one, Jason". The third king had obliged. The drama had concluded with the children singing *O Little Town of Bethlehem*, accompanied by the loud chomping of the Magi.

Mrs Golightly, hearing this surfeit of comment and criticism, stiffened and narrowed her eyes. "Well thank you very much for all those helpful suggestions," she remarked sarcastically. "It is always good to be told how things could be improved."

"Don't take it the wrong way, Bertha," said Miss Tranter. "I was only offering some constructive criticism. After all, I do know something about acting."

"Well, I am sure things will be fine this year, Mrs

Joy is what happens to us when we allow ourselves to

Golightly," interjected the vicar reassuringly and observing the fixed expression on the infant teacher's face. "I am so grateful for all the time and effort you have put in and I know that the children will be splendid."

Mr Pendlebury was not a man who liked any sort of confrontation and he could see that this exchange between the two teachers could escalate unless he intervened. Having said that, after the previous year's performance, he felt decidedly apprehensive and could not resist one final comment:

"Oh, and could the children get the word right for the carol? We don't want a repetition of last year when they sang The First O Hell!"

Mrs Golightly pulled a face. "I shall bear that in mind, Vicar," she said tetchily and wondering to herself why she had let herself in for this.

(from* The School at the Top of the Dale*)

---

recognise how good things really are. — Marianne Williamson

"During one nativity play in a Yorkshire Dales school, the youngster playing Joseph (from a farming background) strode confidently on to the stage. He was a stocky little boy with apple-red cheeks, a round moon face and was attired in a Care Bear dressing gown, blue socks and a tea towel held in place by an elastic belt with a snake clasp. He sported a pair of white trainers with red stripes.

'Hello Joseph,' said Mary cheerfully. 'Have you been working in your carpenter's shop?'

'Aye, I 'ave – an' I'm knackered,' announced the child.

There came the voice off-stage of the teacher. 'Tired!' she said in a loud whisper. 'You're tired'."

Carole Frost

Having somewhere to go is home; having someone to

"When the Magi put in an appearance during the nativity play, galumphing round on invisible camels before dismounting to tether and water their mounts (these Dales children were savvy about animal husbandry), we were surprised to see only two of them.

'I've brought gift of gold,' bellowed the first king, producing a Kit Kat wrapped in gilt foil.

'I've brought gift of Frankincense,' said the second king, brandishing a bottle of his mother's eau de cologne.

Then in unison they announced: 'T'other king, 'e would 'ave brought t' myrrh, but 'e's poorly wi' t' measles.'"

Mary Sheepshanks

Now thrice welcome Christmas,
Which brings us good cheer,
Minc'd pies and plum-porridge,
Good ale and strong beer.

"Women do not consider the following to be Christmas gifts: diet books, cooking utensils, cleaning products, petrol for the car, anything from the Pound Shop."

Jeff Green

When I was sixteen I agreed to accompany Judy, a girl who I met through the Youth Theatre, to the Rotherham Girls' High School Christmas Dance. This was held in the school hall — a dark, cold place which smelled of floor polish and cabbage. It had been decorated with sprigs of holly and trimmings, pictures of snowy landscapes and other festive scenes to brighten the place up, but still looked and smelled like a school hall. There was, of course, no mistletoe.

It was a decorous affair and the girls had been warned by the headmistress in a special assembly to wear appropriate outfits: three-quarter-length dresses, low heels and no plunging necklines. Boys should wear ties and sober jackets and come with a formal invitation, otherwise they would be refused entry. Some teachers observed proceedings with eagle eyes from the vantage point of the hall balcony, whilst others stalked the floor.

The dancing was of the ballroom variety and included the Gay Gordons, the Military Two-Step, the Progressive Barn Dance and the waltz. It must have looked comical, big, strapping lads with slicked-back hair and acne galloping, spinning, twirling their partners and then, for the waltz, shuffling around the floor treading on feet.

The waltz was an opportunity for us to make contact with our partners. We were told by the teachers prior to the music starting that the boy was allowed to encircle a girl's waist but must keep his partner at arm's length, a full yard apart. Inevitably, as soon as the music started, we pulled the girl in close so our bodies touched — until we were spotted by a hawk-faced teacher who soon put a stop to that.

---

and realise they were the big things. — anon

Like many students wanting to earn some extra money, when I was in the sixth form I worked on the post during the Christmas holidays. This was my first experience of the world of work apart from the paper round. The Post Office employed casual labour at this time of year to help deliver the vast quantity of cards, posters, calendars and parcels and, along with many other students, I arrived early at the Central Post Office in Rotherham to be assigned a patch.

My area was Brinsworth, a part of Rotherham I came to know very well, for four years later I was to secure my first teaching position when qualified as an assistant teacher of English at the purpose-built Brinsworth High School. Brinsworth was one of the most desirable rounds, a short bus ride away from the town centre and blessedly free of hills and isolated dwellings. It was a densely-populated area of well-kept semi-detached houses, older, more modest

People are generally about as happy as

terraces and council-owned prefabricated structures, so I didn't have a long trek. There was a small arcade of shops and the one public house, The Three Magpies.

At one house where I was to deliver a calendar, the door was answered by a small boy in vest and underpants.

"Is your mummy in?" I asked him. He shook his head.

"Is your daddy in?" There was another shake of the head.

"Is there anyone else in besides you?" I asked.

"There's our Joan," he told me.

I gave my wife a brand-new watch for Christmas — waterproof, shockproof, unbreakable, and antimagnetic. Absolutely nothing could happen to it. She lost it.
Milton Berle

---

they're willing to be. — Abraham Lincoln

"Could you go and get her?"
"No."
"Why?'
"I can't lift her out of the cot."

"Clever food is not appreciated at Christmas. It makes the little ones cry and the old ones nervous."

Oliver Wendell Holmes

The butcher was closing his shop on Christmas Eve after a busy and stressful day when a woman arrived.

"I'm terribly sorry," she said, "but I wonder if you still have a turkey? I know I've left it dreadfully late but we were to stay with my sister over Christmas. She is ill and I have to cook the dinner. I am without a turkey."

The butcher sighed. "I still have a turkey, I think."

The customer was shown into the shop and the butcher disappeared into the back room, returning a moment later with a turkey which he placed on the scales. It was the very last one.

"That's an eight-pound bird," he told the customer.

"I wonder if you have a larger one?" asked the woman. "You see, there will be quite a lot coming to dinner."

The butcher, with the turkey, retired to the back of the shop. Taking a two-pound iron weight, he pushed it up the back of the bird and then returned to the counter. He placed the bird on the scales.

"This one is a ten-pound bird," he said.

"Oh, that's splendid," exclaimed the woman. "I'll take them both."

---

for what it lacks in length. — Robert Frost

The vicar's wife was walking up the path to the rectory from morning service when she caught sight of a small figure placing some flowers on a grave.

"Hello Daniel," she said.

"'Ello Miss," replied the boy.

"You come here quite often, don't you?" she said. "I've seen how well you look after your grandfather's grave. There's always fresh flowers."

"Aye, I do come regular, Miss." He pointed to the flowers. "These are called Christmas roses and they were one of mi granddad's favourite flowers."

"Actually they are called hellebores and they are amongst my favourites too," the vicar's wife told him. "They bloom very early and they like the shade. You could plant some around your grandfather's grave. There's a legend surrounding the hellebores, you know. My husband mentioned it in one of his sermons. When a small girl went to see Baby Jesus in the stable all those years ago she saw that the shepherds and the kings had taken Him presents. She had nothing to give and began to weep. The tears fell upon the snow and where they had fallen the hellebore grew and the pure white flowers bloomed. It's a lovely story, isn't it?"

Danny was staring up open-mouthed. He looked down at the grave, bent and touched the white petals which lay on the top. "Aye, it is," he said.

***(from* Trouble at the Little Village School)**

I was a member of the OFSTED team inspecting a secondary school. At our first meeting the lead inspector explained that since there was no music specialist on the team, the music department would not be inspected. At the second meeting he informed us that the headteacher had requested that the music department be looked at since the head of department would be retiring at the end of term

---

we could have a pretty good time. — Edith Wharton

after thirty years in the school. The music department, she told the lead inspector, was the most popular and successful in the school and she was certain that the inspectors would discover little with which to find fault.

"It would be so good," she continued, "for Mr Davies to finish his career on a high."

"So someone," said the lead inspector, "has to inspect music. Any volunteers?"

We all stared at the floor. Then Derek, a colleague, 'very kindly' suggested that I might do it.

"I mean, you like music, Gervase," he told me. "You play the piano and have sung in opera."

"I am at the level of a Grade 5," I replied, "and have sung in Gilbert and Sullivan comic operettas, and then only the patter songs of the Major General and Sir Joseph Porter."

"Well it looks as if you will be inspecting music," said the lead inspector.

"Thank you very much, Derek," I said sardonically.

So I arrived at the music room to find Mr Davies waiting.

"Mr Phinn," he said, smiling, "it's so good to see you. I gather you are quite a musician. I believe you sing in opera. Were you trained at the Royal Academy?"

"No, no," I told him, cursing Derek under my breath.

"The Royal College? Guildhall? Royal Northern College?"

"I'm afraid not."

"What instrument do you play?"

"The piano."

"Splendid!" exclaimed Mr Davies. "I wonder if I could prevail upon you to accompany the school choir at our final rehearsal for the Christmas concert? The accompanist has not been able to make it today and..."

"Let me stop you there, Mr Davies," I interrupted. "School inspectors do not take a part in the lesson. They watch and assess."

I have been happy all my life. — Arthur Marshall

"It wouldn't be in a lesson," I was told. "It's lunchtime rehearsal and it's just a few carols, pretty easy to play."

So I was dragooned into becoming the accompanist.

The school choir assembled in the hall and I sat rather nervously at the piano. Fortunately I had played the first piece before. The carol featured a solo, performed beautifully in a high, clear voice by a boy soprano of eleven. He was accompanied by the other children. He sang:

O holy night, the stars are brightly shining
It is the night of our dear Saviour's birth
Long lay the world in sin and error pining
Till He appeared and the soul felt its worth
A thrill of hope the weary world rejoices
For yonder breaks a new glorious morn
Fall on your knees
O hear the angels' voices
O night divine

O night when Christ was born
O night divine o night
O night divine

On the evening of the carol concert I was thankfully relieved of my role as the accompanist made her appearance. I sat with my colleagues and enjoyed a most marvellous programme of carols and readings. It came to the climax of the concert. The young boy soprano began to sing:

O holy night, the stars are brightly shining
It is the night of our dear Saviour's birth...

Then his voice suddenly broke and from his mouth came a most dreadful-sounding croaking and cracking. The boy stopped and looked like a rabbit caught in the headlights' glare. His bottom lip began to tremble. Then something quite wonderful happened. Members of the choir moved forward and surrounded the boy. A girl and a boy rested their hands on the boy's shoulders and the whole choir took

---

descend into the bunker of the family. — Byron Rogers

over the tune. There were few dry eyes in the audience that evening.

The music department was judged to be outstanding and a beaming Mr Davies approached me as I was leaving the school.

"Thank you so much, Mr Phinn," he said. "It has been a pleasure meeting you and I have to say that I was so relieved that I had an inspector who knew about my subject. So, tell me, at which music college did you study?"

A lovely thing about Christmas is that it's compulsory, like a thunderstorm, and we all go through it together.
Garrison Keillor